Little Children's Bible Books

PETER

BROADMAN
&HOLMAN
PUBLISHERS

PETER

Published in 2000 by Broadman & Holman Publishers,
Nashville, Tennessee

Text copyright © 2000 Anne de Graaf
Illustration copyright © 2000 José Pérez Montero
Design by Ben Alex
Conceived, designed and produced by Scandinavia Publishing House
Printed in Hong Kong
ISBN 0-8054-2189-0

Dedicated to Pedro Pérez Rollán and Peter Glennon

There once was a fisherman named Peter. Before he met Jesus though, his name was Simon.

7

Jesus said to Simon,
"Don't be afraid.
Come, follow me."
Jesus chose Simon
plus eleven other
men to be his closest
followers, or
apostles.

Simon and the other apostles followed Jesus from village to village, listening and learning.

The crowds grew larger every time Jesus taught. "Follow me," he called to the people.

Play follow-the-leader. March around the room, then turn around. Now who's following?

13

Simon watched Jesus help
the blind people to see and
the disabled to walk.
Simon could not believe
his eyes.

15

Simon followed Jesus for over two years. The more he learned, the more he wanted to know about Jesus. Simon asked, "Who is Jesus?"

One day Jesus asked his apostles, "Tell me, who do the people say I am?"

Simon let out his breath as Jesus answered, "Ah, Simon, you could only know this from my Father in heaven. Your name is Simon, but from now on you will be called Peter."

Jesus said, "Someday you will lead the people who follow me. They are my church. You will become the rock, or foundation, on which the church is built."

Peter means "Rock." Hold a rock in your hand. What does it feel like?

Once, Jesus helped his apostles catch some fish. Then Jesus asked three times, "Peter do you love me?" Each time Peter answered, "Yes."

Can you tell Jesus you love him? Jesus wanted Peter to help take care of the people who loved Jesus.

After Jesus went back to heaven, his friends were praying. Suddenly, a sound like a strong wind filled the house.

"Whoosh!" It was God's Holy Spirit, come to make Jesus' followers strong and brave! Whisper "Whoosh!"

29

Peter said, "We must tell more people about Jesus!" The people of the city all came from many different countries. Yet when Peter spoke, God helped them understand him!

Jesus' enemies arrested Peter. They had Peter chained to a soldier so he couldn't get away.

Peter wasn't afraid. Peter slept, and trusted Jesus to take care of him. When you sleep, Jesus takes care of you, too.

That night, when Peter opened his eyes, he saw a bright angel! "Hurry!" the angel said. "Get up and come with me!" As the angel spoke, the chains fell off Peter's arms!

When Peter walked right past the snoring guard, what did he hear?

Peter followed Jesus, and spent the rest of his life helping others follow Jesus. He led the Christians bravely. Peter became a true fisher of men.

A NOTE TO THE big PEOPLE:

The *Little Children's Bible Books* may
be your child's first introduction to the
Bible, God's Word. This book about Peter makes the four
Gospels, the Acts of the Apostles and his letters spring to life.
This is a DO book. Point things out and ask your child to find,
seek, say, and discover.

Before you read these stories, pray that your child's
little heart would be touched by the love of God. These stories
are about planting seeds, having vision, learning right from
wrong, and choosing to believe. Pray together after you read
this. There's no better way for big people to learn from little
people.

A little something fun is said in italics by the narrating animal to make the story come alive. In this DO book, wave, wink, hop, roar, or do any of the other things the stories suggest so this can become a fun time of growing closer.

38